Healing From the Loss of a Loved One

A Daily Devotional

Biblion Publishing LLC.

Healing From the Loss of a Loved One

A Daily Devotional

Biblion Publishing LLC.

Healing From the Loss of a Loved One

Biblion Publishing LLC

 Unless otherwise indicated, scripture quotations are taken from the Holy Bible, especially, the New International Version, King James Version, Legacy Standard Bible and English Standard Version.

First Edition / First Printing

Getting the most out of

"Healing From the Loss of a Loved One"

Are you ready to begin the healing process from the loss of a loved one? Do you want to walk in the peace, joy, and restoration that God has provided for you? Do you need a daily guide and reading plan to get you to a new place of healing from your loss? If you answered yes to any of these questions, this devotional is for you! "*Healing From the Loss of a Loved One*" will take you on a journey to realize the restoration that God has ordained for you to walk in right now! Each day presents a scripture reference, a deeper passage section, a personal prayer guide, a sharing of emotions segment, a plan of action, and reflections for each devotion. *"Healing From the Loss of a Loved One"* will help you reach a new level of healing and trust in a faithful God! You will learn new ways to stay motivated and inspired. You will walk in a newness of joy, peace, contentment, abundance, and restoration as you complete each daily guide and reading plan in this devotional. Get ready to be healed beyond what you can think or imagine as you begin to possess a new level of peace, comfort, and joy in the healing power of Christ!

Biblion Publishing LLC.

Dedication

To my daddy, Anthony T. Pleasant, who was a perfect example to me of what a man should be. I miss you so much and love you with all of my heart!

To my mother, Bertha Pleasant; you loved me so much and laid the foundation for my financial success! I can't wait to see you again!

To my pulchritudinous wife Kimberly, and my children Christian, Zion, and Nacara.

To the New Zion Christian Church Family. You are a true blessing in my life!

Humbly Yours in Christ,

Apostle Jamie T. Pleasant

Healing From the Loss of a Loved One

Devotional Synopsis

Congratulations on purchasing this devotional! Get ready to be healed through your daily reading of this devotional. This devotional is filled with scriptures, prayers, and commentaries that God Yahweh personally spoke to me to share with you. This devotional will guide you into a deeper revelation of God's plan for restoring you and allowing you to be able to live a restored and healed life beginning now!

Preface

As the only child from the marriage of Anthony and Bertha Pleasant, I experienced death at a very young age. My mother died when I was twelve years old. I still remember when I was called into the principal's office that morning, where my dad looked at me with tears in his eyes and said she had died. Consequently, my father died when I was a freshman in college. I remember that day when he passed as well. I will never forget seeing him the day before he died, and I shared with him that I loved him and that I would make something out of my life to make him proud of me. He shed a single tear from his right eye and uttered indistinguishable words to me. The following morning, at 1:35 a.m., he departed this earthly life. I felt so alone, and I still remember as I watched his casket go to the ground, as I said to myself, "There goes the last person that will ever be concerned about your well-being." I knew I had to become more serious about life, and I knew I couldn't afford to fail at anything because I had nothing or no one to fall back on. I immediately began to work harder and became overly serious about everything in life. However, as time went on, I became depressed and worn out because I was doing everything on my own. Shortly thereafter, I began to seek Jesus Christ. One day, I stumbled into a church and cried through the entire service but noticed that I felt so much better. Shortly after, I gave my life to Christ, began reading His word, and all of my anxieties, depression, and sadness went away. Christ Jesus healed me of the negative effects of losing the two most precious people in my life. I never looked back and have been walking in joy and peace for over thirty years. By writing this devotion, I hope it will have the same impact as Christ and his word had on me. I pray for your healing, joy, restoration, and peace. In Christ, Amen.

23 Buy truth, and do not sell it;
buy wisdom, instruction, and
understanding.

Proverbs 23:23 (ESV)

This Devotional Belongs To

Day 1

Jesus wept. (John 11:35, ESV)

Deeper Look

This passage of scripture shows us that Jesus, the Son of God, wept. Don't let anyone ever tell you that you shouldn't cry when a loved one has passed. Crying is a powerful emotion that Yahweh has given us to alleviate the pain we are experiencing. experiencing from our loss.

Personal Prayer

Lord Yahweh, thank you for letting me know that it is alright to cry at the passing of a loved one. Give me the strength to go through this difficult time and begin the healing process. In Christ, I thank you. Amen.

Emotions I Am Experiencing

1.____________________________________

2.____________________________________

3.____________________________________

4.____________________________________

5.____________________________________

Reflections

Plan of Action

Day 2

"Blessed are those who mourn, for they shall be comforted." (Matthew 5:4, ESV)

Deeper Look

This scripture gives us a reassuring promise that when we experience the loss of a loved one, God Yahweh will also provide comfort for us. He will console us at our deepest level of hurt. He will identify our pain and grief and remove it for sure.

Personal Prayer

Lord, I am hurting right now and need your comfort. I am standing on your promise that you will take away this pain that is deep within my body, mind and soul. I want to feel whole again.

Emotions I Am Experiencing

1.________________________________

2.________________________________

3.________________________________

4.________________________________

5.________________________________

Reflections

Plan of Action

Day 3

The LORD is near to the brokenhearted and saves the crushed in spirit." (Psalm 34:18, ESV)

Deeper Look

This scripture provides peace for us knowing that in our brokenness, He becomes nearer to us than ever before. You should never be hesitant in pouring your heart out to Him, sharing all of your pain. The more you share, the closer He is to you.

Personal Prayer

Lord, I am pouring out my heart to you and letting you know how broken I am right now. The loss of my loved one has left a void in my entire being. I ask you to fill me with your love right now. In Christ, Amen.

Emotions I Am Experiencing

1.____________________________________

2.____________________________________

3.____________________________________

4.____________________________________

5.____________________________________

Reflections

Plan of Action

Day 4

For everything there is a season, and a time for every matter under heaven: a time to weep, and a time to laugh; a time to mourn, and a time to dance;"
(Ecclesiastes 3:1, 4 ESV)

Deeper Look

Crying and feeling sad should only be for a season. Just as there are four seasons on the earth, there are also four seasons in life. There is a season to mourn, as well as to laugh. There is a time to grieve, as well as dance. Avoid being stuck in one season. Experience all four of them. Find something to smile and laugh.

Personal Prayer

Lord Yahweh, I know that mourning for the loss of my loved one should only be a season. I am praying to you now to give me the strength to go on to a season of joy and wholeness. I trust you. In Christ, Amen.

Emotions I Am Experiencing

1.______________________________

2.______________________________

3.______________________________

4.______________________________

5.______________________________

Reflections

Plan of Action

Day 5

...Weeping may endure for the night, but joy cometh with the morning." (Psalm 30:5, KJV)

Deeper Look

This scripture shows us that after a period of weeping, joy is on its way. We determine the length of our nighttime darkness filled with grief and the time that morning will come and dawn us a daylight of joy. Expect your morning to end your mourning. Expect joy to eradicate your grief. God will and shall bring sunshine to you!

Personal Prayer

Lord Yahweh, I want to experience joy again. I am ready for my darkness to turn into a bright and shining day filled with joy. Move in my heart now so that I can see the coming of your glory. In Christ, Amen.

Emotions I Am Experiencing

1.______________________________

2.______________________________

3.______________________________

4.______________________________

5.______________________________

Reflections

Plan of Action

Day 6

Then his servants said to him, "What is this thing that you have done? You fasted and wept for the child while he was alive; but when the child died, you arose and ate food. (2 Samuel 12:21, ESV)

Deeper Look

What a profound proclamation by King David! He shows us how God Yahweh can give us the strength to snap back into the flow of life with vigor and confidence. God Yahweh is a restorer to those of us that are struggling from the loss of a loved one. We should always show the world our faith in His restoration power during rough times.

Personal Prayer

Lord Yahweh, I want to be able to bounce back with vigor in the same way King David did at the loss of his son. I want to be an example to others that I believe in your ability to restore my joy and peace. In Christ, Amen.

Emotions I Am Experiencing

1.________________________________

2.________________________________

3.________________________________

4.________________________________

5.________________________________

Reflections

Plan of Action

Day 7

Jesus said to her, "I am the resurrection and the life. Whoever believes in me, though he die, yet shall he live," (John 11:25, ESV)

Deeper Look

We need to grasp the power in the statement that Jesus has made here. He is saying that death is not a cessation of life. It is the beginning and continuation of a better life that your departed loved one is experiencing right now. Your loved one is in a place that brings them joy, peace and bliss in the presence of the Almighty.

Personal Prayer

Lord, thank you for helping me realize that death is not the end of the existence of my loved one. I have peace knowing that they are in a blissful and beautiful place with you right now. In Christ, Amen.

Emotions I Am Experiencing

1.____________________

2.____________________

3.____________________

4.____________________

5.____________________

Reflections

Plan of Action

Day 8

We are confident, I say, and willing rather to be absent from the body, and to be present with the Lord. (2 Corinthians 5:8, KJV)

Deeper Look

Paul shares a revelation with us here about how our loved ones view death after they depart from the earth. Paul went to heaven and tells us that he confidently wants us to know that if our loved ones were given a choice to return to us on earth, they would choose heaven over us. The Lord's glory is far better than being here on earth.

Personal Prayer

Lord, thank you for showing me that though I miss my loved one here on earth, they however, would prefer to be in your glorious presence experiencing a new life. Help me to celebrate their newfound existence in heaven. In Christ, Amen.

Emotions I Am Experiencing

1.______________________________

2.______________________________

3.______________________________

4.______________________________

5.______________________________

Reflections

Plan of Action

Day 9

My sheep hear my voice, and I know them, and they follow me. I give them eternal life, and they will never perish, and no one will snatch them out of my hand." (John 10:27–28, ESV)

Deeper Look

Here we see that when Jesus calls us, we will always come to Him. Our loved ones heard His call to come be with Him in heaven and they dropped everything on the earth and followed the divine call of eternity. It's a call that is so peaceful and divine that no one can resist it. He called our loved ones to an abundance of eternal peace and joy.

Personal Prayer

Lord, what a blessing it is to understand that my loved one heard your divine call and preferred it over every other voice in the universe. I now see that you have prepared an abundance of joy and peace for them in a very special place. In Christ, Amen.

Emotions I Am Experiencing

1.______________________________________

2.______________________________________

3.______________________________________

4.______________________________________

5.______________________________________

Reflections

Plan of Action

Day 10

"Let not your heart be troubled; you believe in God, believe also in Me. In My Father's house are many mansions; if it were not so, I would have told you. I go to prepare a place for you. And if I go and prepare a place for you, I will come again and receive you to Myself; that where I am, there you may be also." (John 14:1–3, NKJV)

Deeper Look

There is no need to worry about where your loved one is right now. Jesus assures us that He has prepared plenty of rooms for all believers to come and abide in until the new heaven and new earth are revealed. He assures us that not only has He prepared a place for us, but He will also come back and lead all of us to that place when it is our time to leave this earth.

Personal Prayer

Lord, I am glad to know that my loved one is in a prepared special place that was reserved by Christ. It is wonderful to think that they are enjoying the beauty and comfort of heaven. In Christ, Amen.

Emotions I Am Experiencing

1.____________________________________

2.____________________________________

3.____________________________________

4.____________________________________

5.____________________________________

Reflections

Plan of Action

Day 11

And he said, "Jesus, remember me when you come into your kingdom." And he said to him, "Truly, I say to you, today you will be with me in paradise."" (Luke 23:42–43, ESV)

Deeper Look

What a great revelation to know that the second our loved ones depart this life, they are immediately in paradise with Christ! There is no cessation of awareness of their existence. They immediately transfer to a new reality that is filled with love, joy and peace. What a wonderful revelation to know that they are very much alive!

Personal Prayer

Lord Yahweh, how peaceful it is for me to know that my loved one is in a better place with you. I am glad to know that they are simply continuing life in a new dimension of peace, love and joy. In Christ, Amen.

Emotions I Am Experiencing

1.______________________________

2.______________________________

3.______________________________

4.______________________________

5.______________________________

Reflections

Plan of Action

Day 12

Then Jesus, calling out with a loud voice, said, "Father, into your hands I commit my spirit!" And having said this he breathed his last." (Luke 23:46, ESV)

Deeper Look

Here we see that when our loved ones take their last breath, it is because they have committed their spirt to God Yahweh. They have entrusted their entire being to Him. They know now that He will care for and protect them as they transition to their new home in heaven. You should have peace knowing this truth about death.

Personal Prayer

Lord Yahweh, thanks for showing me that you will not allow a person to take their last breath until you assure them that you will protect and care for them in the next phase of their journey in eternity. Thanks for showing me this! In Christ, Amen.

Emotions I Am Experiencing

1.____

2.____

3.____

4.____

5.____

Reflections

Plan of Action

Day 13

For I am sure that neither death nor life, nor angels nor rulers, nor things present nor things to come, nor powers, nor height nor depth, nor anything else in all creation, will be able to separate us from the love of God in Christ Jesus our Lord." (Romans 8:38–39, ESV)

Deeper Look

Nothing can separate our loved ones, from the love that God Yahweh has for them. As they have departed this life, they are now experiencing the love of Christ at a new level. His love is engulfing them and leading them to a new reality that is far better than any love they have ever experienced from anyone here on earth.

Personal Prayer

Lord Yahweh, you know how I love this person that has passed from this earth to heaven. I know now that as strong as my love is for them, it doesn't compare to the love they are experiencing from you right now. Your love is far more encompassing! In Christ, Amen.

Emotions I Am Experiencing

1.______________________________

2.______________________________

3.______________________________

4.______________________________

5.______________________________

Reflections

Plan of Action

Day 14

and everyone who lives and believes in me shall never die. Do you believe this? (John 11:26, ESV)

Deeper Look

The question Jesus wants to know is: "Do you believe that when you are a Christian, you will never die?" If you hold this belief, you can be certain that your loved one is alive and well. They are cognizant of everything going on at this very moment. They are experiencing a reality that words can't explain. There is peace and joy all around them.

Personal Prayer

Lord, I now know that death is not the end. It is a continuation of life in a new dimension. I am beginning to change my attitude towards death as I now view it as an extension of life in a new dimension. Praise your name Lord. In Christ, Amen.

Emotions I Am Experiencing

1.______________________________

2.______________________________

3.______________________________

4.______________________________

5.______________________________

Reflections

Plan of Action

Day 15

Even though I walk through the valley of the shadow of death, I will fear no evil, for you are with me; your rod and your staff, they comfort me." (Psalm 23:4, ESV)

Deeper Look

Don't let the shadow of death cloud the sunshine of life that Yahweh has in store for you. The aftereffects of death can be brutal, but you should know that He has provided comfort for you in this time of missing your loved one. Remember that death creates a shadow, signifying its passing. Allow it to pass by.

Personal Prayer

Lord, please help me get out of this shadow of death that I am experiencing with the loss of my loved one. Help me walk through this troubling time with the comfort of knowing that you are going to restore me to a place of peace and joy. In Christ, Amen.

Emotions I Am Experiencing

1.______________________________

2.______________________________

3.______________________________

4.______________________________

5.______________________________

Reflections

Plan of Action

Day 16

This is my comfort in my affliction, that your promise gives me life." (Psalm 119:50, ESV)

Deeper Look

You can find peace in the assurance that God Yahweh's comfort instills new life in you. After experiencing the loss of a loved one, anticipate a fresh start in life. Expect God Yahweh to renew your outlook on life to see His goodness like you have never seen before. He is faithful and will do it!

Personal Prayer

Lord, I am ready to step into a newness of life that is positive and full of greatness according to your promise of providing comfort to me. I want to see all the great things you have planned for me as I look into a new season of life. In Christ, Amen.

Emotions I Am Experiencing

1.____

2.____

3.____

4.____

5.____

Reflections

Plan of Action

Day 17

My flesh and my heart may fail, but God is the strength of my heart and my portion forever." (Psalm 73:26, ESV)

Deeper Look

Yahweh wants you to know that He has allotted the perfect amount of peace, joy and restoration that you will need during this time. He is the perfect portion for all of your problems. He pours peace into you in times of turmoil. He pours joy into you when you are sad. And He pours restoration into you when you are worn down.

Personal Prayer

Lord, I am empty right now. Pour peace in my disarrayed state. Pour joy in my state of mourning. Pour restoration in my broken and empty vessel. I need a fresh pouring of your anointing in my life right now. In Christ, Amen.

Emotions I Am Experiencing

1.______________________________

2.______________________________

3.______________________________

4.______________________________

5.______________________________

Reflections

Plan of Action

Day 18

For to me to live is Christ, and to die is gain." (Philippians 1:21, ESV)

Deeper Look

Yahweh wants you to know that when a loved one dies, even though it is a loss to us, it is gain for them. They gain an eternal peaceful place to live. They gain joy that is unspeakable and unshakeable. They gain love that can't be described by a million tongues. They gain the goal of their faith, which is life everlasting!

Personal Prayer

Lord, I rejoice in the fact that my view about death is really changing. I truly believe that when we lose a loved one, they have gained the ultimate goal of their faith, which is, eternal life that brings joy, peace and completeness! In Christ, Amen.

Emotions I Am Experiencing

1.____________________________________

2.____________________________________

3.____________________________________

4.____________________________________

5.____________________________________

Reflections

Plan of Action

Day 19

Precious in the sight of the LORD is the death of his saints." (Psalm 116:15, ESV)

Deeper Look

How precious a is deceased loved one to God Yahweh. He says that when a loved one dies, it is a precious sight to Him because we belong to Him through the salvation of Christ! Get excited to know that God views your loved one preciously the moment they transition in His presence. What a blessing to be viewed that way by Him!

Personal Prayer

Lord, I am so excited to know that you view death so differently from us here on earth. We are sad when we view a body in a coffin. You view that same coffin and see nothing but a precious saint that Has come into your presence. Wow! In Christ, Amen.

Emotions I Am Experiencing

1.______________________________________

2.______________________________________

3.______________________________________

4.______________________________________

5.______________________________________

Reflections

Plan of Action

Day 20

But we do not want you to be uninformed, brothers, about those who are asleep, that you may not grieve as others do who have no hope. For since we believe that Jesus died and rose again, even so, through Jesus, God will bring with him those who have fallen asleep. (1 Thessalonians 4:13–14, ESV)

Deeper Look

What a joy to know that God has given us evidence to not grieve the way others do when we lose a loved one. The promise we have that unbelievers don't have is the assurance of hope. We are assured that just as Jesus died and was resurrected, so shall our loved one be resurrected as well. We will all be united with Him on that great day!

Personal Prayer

Lord Yahweh, I receive this promise that you have given me which is, the ability to not grieve the way unbelievers do. They have no hope for the future. My future and loved one's future is anchored in the shed blood of Jesus on the cross! In Christ, Amen.

Emotions I Am Experiencing

1.____________________________________

2.____________________________________

3.____________________________________

4.____________________________________

5.____________________________________

Reflections

Plan of Action

Day 21

Therefore He is able also to save forever those who draw near to God through Him, since He always lives to make intercession for them." (Hebrews 7:25, LSB)

Deeper Look

Salvation is forever! Salvation is a process that began and ended at Calvary. Rest assured that when your loved ones gave their life to Jesus, they were saved completely and forever. To the uttermost He did the work of salvation. Therefore, don't be concerned about their salvation. Once saved, always saved. They are forever saved in His care.

Personal Prayer

Lord Yahweh, It brings great joy to my soul to know that salvation was signed, sealed and delivered to all that believe in Christ as their Lord and Savior. I know that I will see my loved one again very soon as we will all bask in the Lord's presence. In Christ, Amen.

Emotions I Am Experiencing

1. ____________________

2. ____________________

3. ____________________

4. ____________________

5. ____________________

Reflections

Plan of Action

Day 22

Truly, truly, I say to you, whoever hears my word and believes him who sent me has eternal life. He does not come into judgment but has passed from death to life." (John 5:24, ESV)

Deeper Look

When we say someone has passed, it means more than they have died. It means that they have forgone judgment that condemns them and have come under the imputed righteousness of Jesus Christ, where sin has no record of their name. When they pass, they have forgone death and have entered an eternal life of righteousness.

Personal Prayer

Lord Yahweh, I am really growing as I have learned that when we pass, we have exempted judgement from all sin on this earth that we are guilty of. We can only pass from judgement as Jesus is our Lord and Savior who unceasingly intercedes for us daily. In Christ, Amen.

Emotions I Am Experiencing

1.______________________________

2.______________________________

3.______________________________

4.______________________________

5.______________________________

Reflections

Plan of Action

Day 23

For as by a man came death, by a man has come also the resurrection of the dead. For as in Adam all die, so also in Christ shall all be made alive." (1 Corinthians 15:21–22, ESV)

Deeper Look

Because of Adam's sin, death came to us. Because of Jesus' death, life has been given back to us eternally. Jesus rectified all the wrongdoing of the one man, Adam. What a just God we serve. We inherited sin from Adam, and we also have inherited life from Christ. Your loss of a saved loved one is only temporary. You will meet again soon.

Personal Prayer

Lord Yahweh, I can't wait to see my loved one again that has passed from this life. I can't wait until we celebrate our newness in the new heaven and new earth that you have prepared for us. I am excited that my new life is realized in Christ Jesus. In Christ, Amen.

Emotions I Am Experiencing

1.____

2.____

3.____

4.____

5.____

Reflections

Plan of Action

Day 24

I believe that I shall look upon the goodness of the LORD in the land of the living!" (Psalm 27:13, ESV)

Deeper Look

Death can make you think that the world has come to an unhappy and tumultuous end. You may even feel like there is no joy left in this life anymore. However, God Yahweh has promised that you will see the goodness in the land while you are still living. As long as there is breath in your body, He has an exceeding amount of goodness to share with you!

Personal Prayer

Lord Yahweh, the heaviness of the loss of a loved one is real. Give me an anointing to clear my vision so that I can see your goodness on the earth while I am still here. Breathe into my body joy, peace and understanding. In Christ, Amen.

Emotions I Am Experiencing

1.______________________________

2.______________________________

3.______________________________

4.______________________________

5.______________________________

Reflections

Plan of Action

Day 25

And the peace of God, which surpasses all understanding, will guard your hearts and your minds in Christ Jesus." (Philippians 4:7, ESV)

Deeper Look

God has provided peace for you during the time of the loss of your loved one. Don't try to understand why your loved one died or what could have been done to prevent it. Focus on the truth that He has promised to give you a peace that will guard your heart from irreparable damage. His peace will protect your mind from depression as well.

Personal Prayer

Lord, at first I was trying to grapple with why my loved one had to die. Now I am asking you to release peace to me so that I can have a renewed heart and a healthy mind. I need your peace right now Lord, more than ever before. Help me! In Christ, Amen.

Emotions I Am Experiencing

1.______________________________

2.______________________________

3.______________________________

4.______________________________

5.______________________________

Reflections

Plan of Action

Day 26

He will wipe away every tear from their eyes, and death shall be no more, neither shall there be mourning, nor crying, nor pain anymore, for the former things have passed away."" (Revelation 21:4, ESV)

Deeper Look

God has promised to wipe away every tear that death has caused in our lives. He has also said that pain will be no more and will pass away into eternal nonexistence. The day is coming when we will not mourn because of death ever again. We will only shout with joy in perfect union with Christ in a beautiful place on the new earth.

Personal Prayer

Lord, thank you for wiping away my tears after the loss of my loved one. I look forward to the day when there will be no more mourning, crying or pain because of death. I thank you for your love and protection as I go through this rough time in my life. In Christ, Amen.

Emotions I Am Experiencing

1.______________________________

2.______________________________

3.______________________________

4.______________________________

5.______________________________

Reflections

Plan of Action

Day 27

But our citizenship is in heaven, and from it we await a Savior, the Lord Jesus Christ, who will transform our lowly body to be like his glorious body, by the power that enables him even to subject all things to himself." (Philippians 3:20–21, ESV)

Deeper Look

What a blessing to know that our loved ones have simply claimed their citizenship when they pass from this earth. There is a glorious improved body that awaits us in heaven when we are united with Him completely when the resurrection comes. We must be excited for our loved ones that are beginning to experience the newness of their being.

Personal Prayer

Lord, I need a transformation to begin for me right now. Transform my mind, body and soul to trust in you for restoration from the loss of my loved one. I know that you are faithful and will begin the healing process for me now. In Christ, Amen.

Emotions I Am Experiencing

1.______________________________

2.______________________________

3.______________________________

4.______________________________

5.______________________________

Reflections

Plan of Action

Day 28

"O death, where is your victory? O death, where is your sting?"" (1 Corinthians 15:55, ESV)

Deeper Look

Its great news to know that death has no power over us anymore. Death can't defeat us anymore. Death is nothing for us to be afraid of as it has been depleted of wreaking fear and havoc in our lives as it doesn't even have the effect of a sting anymore. When we pass, there is no pain. There is just peace, joy and a blissful existence for all believers.

Personal Prayer

Lord, my view about what it is to experience death has definitely changed. I know now that death is a peaceful and victorious moment that we will experience when we leave this earth. Jesus, thank you for giving us the victory over death. In Christ, Amen.

Emotions I Am Experiencing

1.______________________________

2.______________________________

3.______________________________

4.______________________________

5.______________________________

Reflections

Plan of Action

Day 29

I have fought the good fight, I have finished the race, I have kept the faith." (2 Timothy 4:7, ESV)

Deeper Look

The greatest fight that we will ever encounter is the fight of faith. We must have faith that God will do what He said He would do. We must have faith that He is who He says that He is. We must have faith that Jesus has guaranteed us that we are secure with everlasting life, as we have confessed Him as the Lord and Savior of our lives.

Personal Prayer

Lord Yahweh, I am going to keep the faith to the very end. I confess Jesus as Lord and savior of my life. I have faith that I have received everlasting life through Him. I have faith that you will heal my grieving heart. I have faith I will thrive in this life. In Christ, Amen.

Emotions I Am Experiencing

1.________________________________

2.________________________________

3.________________________________

4.________________________________

5.________________________________

Reflections

Plan of Action

Day 30

Henceforth there is laid up for me the crown of righteousness, which the Lord, the righteous judge, will award to me on that day, and not only to me but also to all who have loved his appearing." (2 Timothy 4:8, ESV)

Deeper Look

Our loved ones received the crown of righteousness when they left this earth. Our loved ones are in right standing with Christ and are receiving the apex of their salvation. Glory to Yahweh, who is the Most High God! We will receive that same crown one day! Glory to Jesus, and thank you, Holy Spirit, for sealing us for salvation.

Personal Prayer

Lord, I praise you and thank you for your son Jesus Christ. I am grateful to be able to receive my crown at the end of my life here on earth. I celebrate and I am also in total peace knowing that my loved one has received the crown of life everlasting! In Christ, Amen.

Emotions I Am Experiencing

1.________________________________

2.________________________________

3.________________________________

4.________________________________

5.________________________________

Reflections

Plan of Action

Epilogue

One of the best ways to experience God's trust at new levels in your life is for you to give your life to Christ Jesus. Repeat these simple words, and it will become a reality. Repeat the following: Lord Christ Jesus, as of this very moment, I accept you as Lord and Savior of my life. I now give my life to you so it can be fashioned for your purpose and glory. God, I believe everything I've said and confessed to you. I know now that I have received everlasting life based on the work that Christ has done and will continue to do in my life. Jesus, thank you for bringing me to this point where I surrender everything to you. It is in the Holy Spirit through Christ Jesus; I say Amen.

Humbly Yours in Christ

Apostle Jamie T. Pleasant

Book Dr. Jamie Pleasant for a Speaking Engagement!

For speaking engagements, please contact Dr. Jamie T. Pleasant at

admin@newzionchristianchurch.org or

678.845.7055

About the Author

Apostle Jamie T. Pleasant, Ph.D., a modern-day polymath, is the founder and Chief Executive Pastor of New Zion Christian Church in Suwanee, Georgia. Additionally, he currently serves as a tenured Full Professor of Marketing at Clark Atlanta University's School of Business. Notably, he is the first faculty member in the university's history to be accepted into Mensa International, the world's largest and oldest high IQ society for individuals who have scored in the 98th percentile or above on an intelligence test.

Dr. Pleasant is the first African American to graduate from the Georgia Institute of Technology (Georgia Tech) with a Ph.D. in Business Management with a concentration in Marketing, earning that degree in August 1999. He is a 2016 recipient of the "Lifetime Achievement Award" from former President Barack Obama of the USA for volunteer and community service. He was awarded the "Game Changer" Educator Award by

Reverend Jesse Jackson at the 2019 Rainbow PUSH International Convention. As a polyhistor, in addition to obtaining a doctorate degree in Business Management from the Georgia Institute of Technology, he holds a bachelor's degree in physics from Benedict College in Columbia, South Carolina, Marketing Studies from Clemson University and an M.B.A. in Marketing from the very prestigious, Clark Atlanta University.

Under his leadership, New Zion has grown from three members when it started in 1995 to well over 700 in weekly attendance, with a focus on economic and entrepreneurial development. God gave him the vision to establish a Biblically based economic development initiative for New Zion Christian Church. He remains at the pulse of the economic business sector in American society.

As a result, Apostle Pleasant is in constant demand to train, speak and teach others at all levels in ministry and the private sector about business and economic development across the country. He has created numerous cutting edge and industry leading ministerial, business and economic development classes and programs, along with SAT & PSAT prep courses for children ages 9-19. He founded The Financial Literacy Academy for Youth (FLAFY), where youth between the ages of 13-19 attend 12-week intense classes on financial money management principles. At the end of those 12 weeks, they receive a "Personal Finance" certificate of achievement. In 2015, he established The Young Leadership and Success Academy that teaches young people between the ages of 10-21 how to invest, make presentations and start and operate businesses. Other ministries he has pioneered include The Wealth Builders Investment Club (WBIC), which educates and allows members to actively invest in the stock market, along with the much-celebrated Institute of Entrepreneurship (IOE), where participants earn a certificate in entrepreneurship after three months of comprehensive training in all aspects of starting and owning a successful competitive business. The main goal and purpose of IOE is that each year one of the trained businesses will be awarded up to $10,000 startup money to ensure financial success.

Apostle Pleasant has met with political officials such as former President Bill Clinton and Nelson Mandela. He has performed marriage ceremonies and counseled numerous celebrated personalities such as Usher Raymond, Terri Vaughn, and many others. Several gospel music artists have performed at the church, including Tiff Joy. Each year, Apostle Pleasant conducts chapel services for Clemson University's football team and is a spiritual and personal friend to its two-time national championship head coach, Dabo Swinney.

As a modern-day civil rights leader, he is a close aide to Reverend Jesse Jackson and serves on the Board of Directors of Rainbow PUSH Inc. (Atlanta) and Director of Business Education and Corporate Engagement. He serves on the Board of Fellowship of Christian Athletes (Atlanta Urban) and after the Columbine High School shooting, he founded the National School Safety Advocacy Association. His latest foundations include the Young Entrepreneurship Program (YEP) and the

African American Consumer Economic Rights (AACER).

He has authored numerous books that include: *Trusting God In Troubling Times, Prayer Changes Things, Powerful Prayers That Open Heaven, Capturing and Keeping the Pastor's Heart, Unshakable Faith, Proverbs for Prosperity, How to release Your Blessings Through Service in Ministry, When Purpose is at Work, Today's Apostles (2024 ed.), Advertising Principles: How to Effectively Reach African Americans in the 21st Century, Discover a New You: A 21 Day Journey to Uncovering Your Uniqueness, Daily Quotes for Daily Blessings, The Making of a Man, I'm Just Sayin', From My Heart To Yours: Love Letters From A Loving Father, Today's Apostle: Servants of God Leading His People towards Unity, A 7 Day Prayer Plan for Prosperity, You Have What It Takes, A Marketing Model for Ethnic Consumer Behavior, An Overview of Strategic Healthcare Marketing and The Importance of Subcultural Marketing.*

Apostle Pleasant is a lifetime member of Alpha Phi Alpha Fraternity Inc. He is the loving husband of the pulchritudinous Kimberly Pleasant and the proud father of three children: Christian, Zion and Nacara.

FINI

Biblion
Publishing L.L.C.

Biblion

Publishing LLC.

BIBLION PUBLISHING

www.ingramcontent.com/pod-product-compliance
Lightning Source LLC
La Vergne TN
LVHW041124061026
849616LV00028B/141